ON THE CAMPAIGN TRAIL

SCANDALS AND BLUNDERS THAT KILLED CAMPAIGNS

VIRGINIA LOH-HAGAN

45TH PARALLEL PRESS

Published in the United States of America by Cherry Lake Publishing Group
Ann Arbor, Michigan
www.cherrylakepublishing.com

Reading Adviser: Beth Walker Gambro, MS, Ed., Reading Consultant, Yorkville, IL
Content Adviser: Mark Richards, Ph.D., Professor, Dept. of Political Science, Grand Valley State University, Allendale, MI
Book Designer: Frame25 Productions

Photo Credits: Harris & Ewing, Library of Congress, Prints and Photographs Division, cover, title page; © wellphoto/Shutterstock, 5; © Andrey_Popov/Shutterstock, 7; John Trumbull, Public domain, via Wikimedia Commons, 9; Created by Adam B. Walter (1820-1875); cropped by Beyond My Ken (talk) 02:14, 15 April 2015 (UTC), Public domain, via Wikimedia Commons, 13; National Archives and Records Administration, Public domain, via Wikimedia Commons, 17; Ollie Atkins, Public domain, via Wikimedia Commons, 19; Bob Chamberlin, Los Angeles Times, CC BY 4.0 via Wikimedia Commons, 21; Vidor, Public domain, via Wikimedia Commons, 25; © Krakenimages.com/Shutterstock, 29; © PeopleImages.com - Yuri A/Shutterstock, 31

Copyright © 2025 by Cherry Lake Publishing Group

All rights reserved. No part of this book may be reproduced or utilized in any form or by any means without written permission from the publisher.

45th Parallel Press is an imprint of Cherry Lake Publishing Group.

Library of Congress Cataloging-in-Publication Data has been filed and is available at catalog.loc.gov

Cherry Lake Publishing Group would like to acknowledge the work of the Partnership for 21st Century Learning, a Network of Battelle for Kids. Please visit Battelle for Kids online for more information.

Note from publisher: Websites change regularly, and their future contents are outside of our control. Supervise children when conducting any recommended online searches for extended learning opportunities.

Printed in the United States of America

ABOUT THE AUTHOR

Dr. Virginia Loh-Hagan is an author and educator. She is currently the Director of the Asian Pacific Islander Desi American (APIDA) Center at San Diego State University and the Co-Executive Director of The Asian American Education Project. She lives in San Diego with her very tall husband and very naughty dogs.

CONTENTS

Introduction 4

Chapter 1: **The Affair That Broke Hamilton (1791)** 8

Chapter 2: **Scandalous Duels and Deals (1805)** 10

Chapter 3: **Caned on the Senate Floor (1856)** 12

Chapter 4: **Bonus Army Against Hoover (1932)** 14

Chapter 5: **Deadly Car Crash (1969)** 16

Chapter 6: **Watergate (1972)** 18

Chapter 7: **Too Many Hearts for Hart (1988)** 20

Chapter 8: **The Wedding Plot (1992)** 22

Chapter 9: **Dean Scream (2004)** 24

Chapter 10: **Emailgate (2016)** 26

Do Your Part! 28

Glossary, Learn More, Index 32

INTRODUCTION

The United States is a top world power. It's not ruled by kings or queens. It's a **democracy**. A democracy is a system of government. It means "rule by the people." People **elect** their leaders. They choose leaders by voting.

Leaders **represent** the people who voted for them. They speak for them. They make decisions for them. That's why voting is so important. By voting, we choose our leaders.

Candidates run for **public office**. Public office is a government position. Candidates work hard to get votes. They run **campaigns**. They do this before an election. Campaigns are planned activities. Some campaigns are easy. Some are hard. And some are full of drama.

Candidates running for office go out and speak to the public. It helps them win voters.

Campaigns have been ruined by **scandals**. Scandals are shameful events. They can be shocking. News outlets love scandals. People love reading about them. Scandals spread. Everyone knows about them. They're entertaining. But they're not good for candidates. **Blunders** also happen. These are mistakes that make candidates look bad.

Candidates want to present a good image. They want to be seen as moral. They want to be seen as smart. Scandals and blunders change what people think. They ruin **reputations**. Reputations are opinions held about people.

Some candidates recover from scandals and blunders. But some have killed political campaigns. There have been many scandals and blunders in U.S. history. This book features some of the most interesting ones!

Most scandals involve breaking the law.

CHAPTER ONE

THE AFFAIR THAT BROKE HAMILTON (1791)

The nation's first major scandal was in 1791. Alexander Hamilton (1757–1804) was a politician. He helped build the nation. He wanted to be president. But a scandal ruined his chances.

Hamilton was married. He had an affair with Maria Reynolds. Reynolds was a married woman. Her husband found out. He demanded that Hamilton pay him a **bribe**. Bribe means to make people do things by giving them money. Hamilton paid him to keep quiet. But people found out.

Hamilton admitted to the affair. He published a pamphlet about it. People were shocked. They lost respect for him.

Alexander Hamilton was in charge of the treasury.
He built our banking system. He's on the $10 bill.

CHAPTER TWO

SCANDALOUS DUELS & DEALS
(1805)

Aaron Burr (1756–1836) is famous for killing Alexander Hamilton. Burr was a leader. He ran for U.S. president. He lost to Thomas Jefferson (1743–1826). He became his vice president. Hamilton had insulted Burr. Burr demanded an apology. Hamilton stayed quiet. So, they **dueled**. Duels are a contest to the death.

Burr wasn't loyal to Jefferson. He traveled west. He made sneaky deals. He wanted to create a new western empire. He wanted to rule it. He was planning to invade. He hired spies. He got military weapons. He recruited an army. He did this in 1805.

Jefferson found out. He arrested Burr. Burr destroyed his own political career. No more elections for him. Burr moved to Europe. He came back to New York. He worked as a lawyer.

WORLD AFFAIRS

Other countries have scandals too. Ferdinand Marcos (1917–1989) was the president of the Philippines. His government was full of scandals. He said he was a war hero. But some think he was lying. He broke laws. He silenced the media. He threatened people. He cheated. He stole money. He abused human rights. People were upset with him.

The next election was held early. Marcos claimed he won. The people knew he didn't. Marcos fled with his family. They went to Hawaii. Imelda Marcos (born 1929) was Marcos' wife. She was the first lady. Together, they stole billions. They had a world record for the largest theft from a government. Imelda is famous in her own right. She spent a lot of money. For example, she bought more than 3,000 pairs of shoes.

CHAPTER THREE

CANED ON THE SENATE FLOOR
(1856)

The Kansas-Nebraska Act was introduced in 1854. Politicians argued. They fought over whether slavery should be allowed in these areas.

Charles Sumner (1811–1874) was a U.S. senator. He was from Massachusetts. He fought against slavery. Andrew Butler (1796–1857) was a U.S. senator. He was from South Carolina. He believed in states' rights. He supported slavery.

Sumner gave a speech. He did this in 1856. He insulted Butler. Preston Brooks (1819–1857) was a congressman. He was Butler's cousin. He beat Sumner on the Senate floor. He used a cane. Sumner almost died.

There was much scandal. Sumner recovered. But this scandal helped fuel the Civil War (1861–1865).

This scandal almost killed Brooks's career. But he was allowed to return to office. He was elected for another term.

CHAPTER FOUR

BONUS ARMY AGAINST HOOVER
(1932)

Herbert Hoover (1874–1964) was a U.S. president from 1929–1933. He served during the Great Depression (1929–1939). This was a hard time. People didn't have jobs.

Veterans are former soldiers. A group formed a Bonus Army. They had fought in World War I (1914–1918). They were promised **bonuses** they hadn't received. A bonus is extra cash. They went to Washington, D.C. They marched. They made camps.

Hoover ordered **evictions**. Evict means to kick out. Hoover sent tanks. He sent troops. Troops used tear gas. They drove the veterans out of town. They burned down their camps. A person died. Others were hurt.

Hoover was blamed for killing war veterans. He lost his reelection for president.

THE IDEAL CANDIDATE

Ideal candidates are role models. Barack Obama (born 1961) was the 44th U.S. president. He has a wife named Michelle. He has 2 daughters. The family had a dog named Bo. The Obamas looked like a wholesome family. They were in the White House for 8 years. They didn't have any personal scandals. No affairs. No cheating. No stealing. Obama made a speech in Boston. He said, "We didn't have a scandal that embarrassed us ... you didn't hear about a lot of drama inside our White House." He made another speech in Las Vegas. He said, "I didn't have scandals, which seems like it shouldn't be something you brag about." He said, "Coming out of the modern presidency without anybody going to jail is really good. It's a big deal." However, there were scandals during his presidency. But Obama's personal life wasn't the subject.

CHAPTER FIVE

DEADLY CAR CRASH
(1969)

Ted Kennedy (1932–2009) was a U.S. senator. The night of July 18, 1969, changed his life. He was in Chappaquiddick. This island is in Massachusetts.

Kennedy had left a party. He was with Mary Jo Kopechne (1940–1969). He was driving a car. He crossed a bridge. He lost control. He crashed into the water. Kennedy escaped. He tried to rescue Kopechne. She was trapped in the car. Kennedy reported the crash the next day. He pleaded guilty for leaving the scene. He almost went to jail for 2 months.

This scandal became national news. It haunted Kennedy's career. He ran for president in 1980. But he was not nominated. He would never be president.

The Kennedys are a famous U.S. family. Ted Kennedy's brother, John F. Kennedy (1917–1963), was the 35th U.S. president.

CHAPTER SIX

WATERGATE
(1972)

On June 17, 1972, 5 men were busted. They got caught breaking into the DNC's headquarters at Watergate. DNC stands for Democratic National Committee. The men were stealing papers. They were bugging phones. They wanted to spy on the DNC. They worked for Richard Nixon (1913–1994). They were trying to help his reelection team. Nixon was president at this time.

An investigation was opened. Nixon was connected to the crime. He covered it up. He was caught on tape. He stepped down. He was the first and only president to **resign**. Resign means to quit. Many of his staff were sent to jail.

This scandal killed Nixon's career. But it also killed Americans' trust in their leaders.

Nixon's goodbye after resigning from office in 1974

CHAPTER SEVEN

TOO MANY HEARTS FOR HART
(1988)

Gary Hart (born 1936) was a U.S. senator. He was from Colorado. He ran for U.S. president. He did this several times. In 1988, he had to drop out. His past caught up to him.

He was campaigning. A newspaper broke a story. It accused Hart of having an affair. Hart was married. He had an affair with Donna Rice (born 1958).

Hart fought back. He denied cheating. He said, "Follow me around." It turns out he was lying. There was too much proof against him. There were other women. Hart let people down. He wasn't what they thought. Voters judged his character.

Journalists spied on Gary Hart. They staked out his house. They took pictures.

CHAPTER EIGHT

THE WEDDING PLOT
(1992)

Ross Perot (1930–2019) was rich. He was a businessman. He was from Texas. He ran for U.S. president. He ran against George H. W. Bush (1924–2018). He did this in 1992.

Perot dropped out of the race. He did this for several weeks. He blamed Bush. He said Bush's team used dirty tricks. He said they threatened to **smear** his daughter. Smear means to lie about.

Perot said Bush's team was planning to publish a fake photo of his daughter. This photo was to be released before her wedding. Perot said, "I cannot prove that any of that happened. I just got reports. It was a risk I could not take." Perot wanted to protect his daughter. His daughter told him to rejoin the race. He still lost.

HOT-BUTTON ISSUE

Hot-button issues refer to tough topics. People have strong emotions. They take sides. Candidates are public figures. Many are famous. They have private lives. Some people think candidates give up their private lives. They think we have a right to know personal details. They judge candidates on their private lives.

Others think candidates have a right to privacy. They don't care about candidates' private lives. They care about their ideas. They care about their actions. Not everyone cares about scandals and blunders. Not everyone agrees on them, either. A scandal or blunder can be a big deal for one person. It can mean nothing to another. Also, scandals and blunders have changed over time. Culture has shifted. Things that were scandalous in the past may not be so today.

CHAPTER NINE

DEAN SCREAM
(2004)

Howard Dean (born 1948) was the governor of Vermont. He ran for U.S. president in 2004. He hoped to win the Democratic Party nomination.

Dean gave a speech. He did this in Iowa. He had too much energy. He excited the crowds. He listed states he'd win. He screamed, "Yeah!" His scream was caught on video. The video went viral.

His scream was called the "Dean Scream." Dean's speech took place on Martin Luther King Jr. Day. Some people called it Dean's "I Have a Scream" speech.

People made fun of Dean. He soon dropped out of the race.

The Dean Scream is the first viral political meme.
Memes are funny images or videos.

CHAPTER TEN
EMAILGATE
(2016)

Hillary Clinton (born 1947) is a politician. She ran for U.S. president. She did this twice. She ran in 2008 and 2016.

In 2016, Clinton ran against Donald Trump (born 1946). Right before election day, there was a big scandal. Clinton had been using her personal email account for government work. This caused security issues.

Trump also had many scandals. He pushed attention away from himself. He focused on Clinton's email scandal. He compared it to Watergate. His supporters chanted, "Lock her up!" Trump ended up winning the election.

FACT-CHECK

It's important to check facts. Facts must be correct. Here are some fun facts about other political scandals:

- Oswaldo López Arellano (1921–2010) was president of Honduras. Honduras is in Central America. He took more than $2 million in bribes. He did this to lower taxes on bananas. He was caught. He was overthrown. The scandal was called "Bananagate." Arellano denied taking bribes.

- Chris Christie (born 1962) was the governor of New Jersey. He ran for U.S. president. In 2013, he closed traffic lanes in Fort Lee. These lanes led to the George Washington Bridge. This closed access to New York City. This happened during rush hour. It caused traffic jams. Some think Christie was punishing Mark Sokolich (born 1963). Sokolich was the mayor of Fort Lee. He did not support Christie's election campaign. Christie denied ordering the closings. He blamed his staff. He fired people. This scandal was called "Bridgegate."

DO YOUR PART!

U.S. citizens have 2 special rights. Only U.S. citizens can vote in federal elections. Only U.S. citizens can run for **federal office**. Federal office means a national office. It's different from state and local offices.

U.S. citizens have many other rights. But they also have duties. The most powerful is the duty to vote. Voting is how people choose leaders. It's how people make changes. It's how people promote their ideas. Those elected make the laws. They make policies. They make the rules. They work for voters.

U.S. citizens can vote at age 18. But people are never too young to get involved in democracy.

Voting is one way Americans can make their voices heard in politics.

Citizens should vote for the best candidate. They should learn about the candidates. But there's a lot of fake news. Citizens should figure out the truth. Here are some ideas to study scandals:

★ Think about the source. Sources are the origins. They started the scandal. Check if the source can be trusted. Check if the source is real.

★ Read beyond the headings. Headings can be flashy. They get attention. Learn the whole story. Do this before judging.

★ Ask an expert. Do research. Learn what others think. Don't trust just one source.

Everyone can do their part. Being a good citizen is hard work. But the work is worth it. Your vote is your voice.

Social media makes it easier to spread fake news.

GLOSSARY

blunders (BLUHN-durz) mistakes made because of carelessness or ignorance

bonuses (BOH-nuhs-iz) amounts of money added to wages or extra pay

bribe (BRYEB) to try to make someone do something by giving them money or gifts

campaigns (kam-PAYNZ) organized courses of action to achieve a goal such as winning an election

candidates (KAN-duh-dayts) people who want to be elected to certain positions

democracy (dih-MAH-kruh-see) a system of government led by voters, often through elected representatives

dueled (DOO-uhld) took part in a contest with deadly weapons arranged between two people to decide an argument

elect (ih-LEKT) to choose someone to hold public office by voting

evictions (i-VIKT-shuhnz) events in which people are legally forced out of their homes

federal office (FEH-druhl AW-fuhs) an elected position in the national government

public office (PUH-blik AW-fuhs) government position established by law

represent (reh-prih-ZENT) to speak or act for another person or group

reputations (reh-pyuh-TAY-shunz) beliefs or opinions generally held about someone or something

resign (rih-ZYEN) to voluntarily leave a job

scandals (SKAN-duhlz) actions or events regarded as morally or legally wrong and causing general public outrage

smear (SMEER) to damage someone's reputation with false accusations

veterans (VEH-tuh-ruhnz) soldiers who have served in the armed forces

LEARN MORE

Books

Goodman, Susan E. *See How They Run: Campaign Dreams, Election Schemes, and the Race to the White House*. New York: Bloomsbury, 2008.

Levy, Elizabeth. *Bringing down a President: The Watergate Scandal*. New York: Roaring Brook Press, 2019.

Shamir, Ruby. *What's the Big Deal about Elections?* New York: Philomel Books, 2018.

INDEX

accidents, 16
Arellano, Oswaldo Lopez, 27
assault, 12

blunders, 6, 23, 24–25
Bonus Army (WWI veterans), 14
bribery, 8, 27
Brooks, Preston, 12–13
Burr, Aaron, 10
Bush, George H.W., 22
Butler, Andrew, 12

Chappaquiddick, Massachusetts, 16
Christie, Chris, 27
Clinton, Hillary, 26
cover-ups, 8, 18

Dean, Howard, 24–25
democracy, 4, 28

email accounts, 26
extramarital affairs, 8, 20–21

Hamilton, Alexander, 8–9, 10
Hart, Gary, 20–21
Hoover, Herbert, 14

illegal activity, 7, 10, 11, 12, 18, 27

Jefferson, Thomas, 10

Kansas-Nebraska Act (1854), 12
Kennedy, Ted, 16–17
Kopechne, Mary Jo, 16

Marcos, Ferdinand and Imelda, 11
media coverage
    investigations, 18, 20–21
    memes, 24–25
    news items, 6, 8, 16
    as political tool, 22

Nixon, Richard, 18–19

Obama, Barack, 15

Perot, Ross, 22
political crimes, 10, 11, 18, 27
presidential hopefuls, 8, 10, 16, 20–21, 22, 24–25, 26, 27
presidents, 10, 11, 14, 15, 17, 18–19, 22, 27
privacy rights, 23

scandals, 6, 15, 23
social media, 24–25, 31
Sumner, Charles, 12

traitors, 10
Trump, Donald, 26

veterans, 14
viral videos, 24–25
voting, 4, 28–30

Watergate (1972), 18–19